The Badass Book for Spiritual Renegades

Your bitchin' book filled with badassery:
Affirmations, colouring pages and more.

by Carla-Jayne Hollingworth

The Badass Book for Spiritual Renegades is a work of my own creation.

The information in this book was correct at the time of publication, and the Author does not assume any liability for loss or damage caused by errors or omissions, again, this is my perspective, opinion, and experience, so it has been written as such.

ISBN - 978-1-961185-00-5

Cover, Book Design, and Layout by Carla-Jayne

www.inomniaparatuspublishing.com

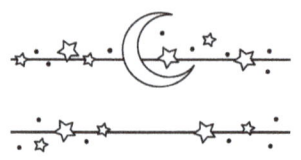

Dedication

I ummed and ahhed about whom I'd most like to dedicate this book to, and when it boils down to it, there's so many people who have inspired and motivated me!

After reflection, what I have found is that it's YOU, dear reader, who inspires me the most. You have taken steps to empower yourself and continue the path of expansion.
And that is fucking magical.

So I am dedicating this book to you my love, and I hope it helps you to do the shit you need to do.
Sending you all the big love and sparkles, beaut!

Introduction

You've picked this book up because you're absolutely a spiritual renegade like me!

A spiritual renegade is someone who has broken free from the constraints of the beliefs that have held them back, they don't give 2 flying fucks about things that don't light them on fire, and they are ready to expand their soul as much as their minds when it comes to their path.

Even if you're not quite there yet, you know you need a kick up the bum to embrace the parts of yourself that this book will help you to reveal.

We're not leaving your inner child out either, with a little outlet through colouring, journaling and inspiration.

This book has been crafted with a smidge of creativity, a dash of sass, a half cup of swears and an overabundance of love and magic.

It is the "book lite" version of my personality.
I am a creative, fierce, slightly feral, intuitive coach and tarot reader ready to help you to empower the shit out of yourself and guide you on your journey.

I stand for being authentic AF and loving what you do with pure passion. If you ask, I'm there in your corner to help you get off the self-haterade.

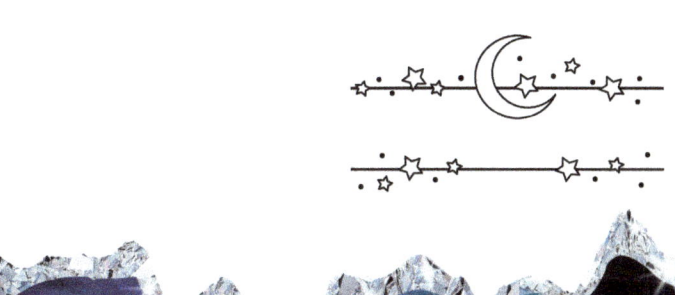

My mission is to equip as many fellow spiritual renegades as possible to overcome BS beliefs without disconnecting from themselves and their higher self so that they live a life of magical ease and abundance.

When I'm not doodling in the margins of notebooks, amassing a collection of sweary oracle cards or glittering something that probably doesn't need to be glittered, you can find me watching my favourite sci-fi programs (I'm a massive Whovian,) travelling the world with my husband Marc, or reading cutesy supernatural stories.

You've heard about me, **I want to hear about you!** I'd love to connect, so why not join my free Facebook community?

https://www.facebook.com/groups/tarotcoachingwithcarla

If you leave a smashing review about this book in there too, I'd love you to receive a free card reading.
(If you hadn't guessed already, I'm British!)
I can't wait to meet you!

Scan to Connect

https://linktr.ee/newleafyourlife

Foreward

I don't need to tell you how to use a journal, but a bitch might just give you some tips on how to best utilise this book.
Firstly, this is printed on thicker style paper, so unless you get watercolour-happy with the colouring pages, the colours shouldn't bleed through massively onto the other side.
Speaking of the other side - this is a bullet journal page where you can use the faint dots to doodle all day long.
I've put both the doodle pages and colouring pages in because sometimes your inner child just wants to colour, dammit!
It's a super healthy yet creative outlet.
And who doesn't love colouring?

Then you have your quotes and affirmations. Please take on what resonates, and leave what doesn't.
The affirmations have been created with the PPEP format: Personal, filled with Positive language, Emotionally connected and in the Present.
Now if you don't like any of the affirmations I've carefully crafted for you, absofuckinlutely make your own using the above format. I teach this in my programs to help empower the shit out of your bad selves!

Then finally you've got some sexy AF notes pages to scribble your innermost thoughts to your heart's content.

Easy, yes?

So go out there and be that badass I know you are!

"The most important relationship you have is the one with yourself."

– Diane von Furstenberg

I am a spiritual badass, connected to the universe and all its energy.

"You don't have to be great to start, but you have to start to be great."

– Zig Ziglar

I'm ready to step up and keep going, even if things get shitty.

"Spirituality is not about being perfect, it's about being authentic."

– Gabrielle Bernstein

I am empowered to create my own reality and I choose to live a life of magic, joy, and wonder.

"Everything in the
universe is within you.
Ask all from yourself."

– Rumi

I am the boss of my life,
and I call the shots.

"The most courageous
act is still to think
for yourself.
Aloud."

– Coco Chanel

I radiate confidence, and
nothing can dull my shine.

"Magic is not a practice. It is a living, breathing web of energy that, with our permission, can encase our every action."

– Dorothy Morrison

I am powerful beyond measure and capable of manifesting my deepest desires.

"Love yourself first and everything else falls into line. You really have to love yourself to get anything done in this world."

– Lucille Ball

I'm worthy of all the wonderful, magical shit the Universe provides.

"Life is like riding a bicycle. To keep your balance, you must keep moving."

– Albert Einstein

I am grateful for all the lessons and experiences that have brought me to this moment.

"You are a child of the universe, no less than the trees and the stars. You have a right to be here."

- Max Ehrmann

I am resilient and capable of overcoming any challenge.

"If you want to find the secrets of the universe, think in terms of energy, frequency, and vibration."

– Nikola Tesla

I embrace my unique gifts and use them to create positive change in the world.

"You are a spiritual being having a human experience."

- Pierre Teilhard de Chardin

I am a vessel for divine energy, using my magic for the highest good of all.

"I'm tough, I'm ambitious, and I know exactly what I want. If that makes me a bitch, okay."

– Madonna

I am a force to be reckoned with, and I will leave my mark on the world with my magic and power.

I don't compare myself to others, I am on my own path

"The present moment is the only moment available to us, and it is the door to all moments."

- Thich Nhat Hanh

I am grateful for today. I am a motherfucking rockstar.

I choose thoughts that create a bright future

"Your task is not to seek for love, but merely to seek and find all the barriers within yourself that you have built against it."

– Rumi

I am a magnet for positive energy and abundance, and I attract only what is in alignment with my highest good.

"You can't be that kid standing at the top of the waterslide, overthinking it. You have to go down the chute."

– Tina Fey

I trust that the universe is always working in my favour, even when things don't go as planned.

I express my feelings when I need to

"I am not afraid of storms,
for I am learning how to
sail my ship."

- Louisa May Alcott

I am capable, confident,
and courageous in all
aspects of my life.

"I have the power to
create my own reality."

– Oprah Winfrey

I am always in control
of my actions,
reactions and thoughts.

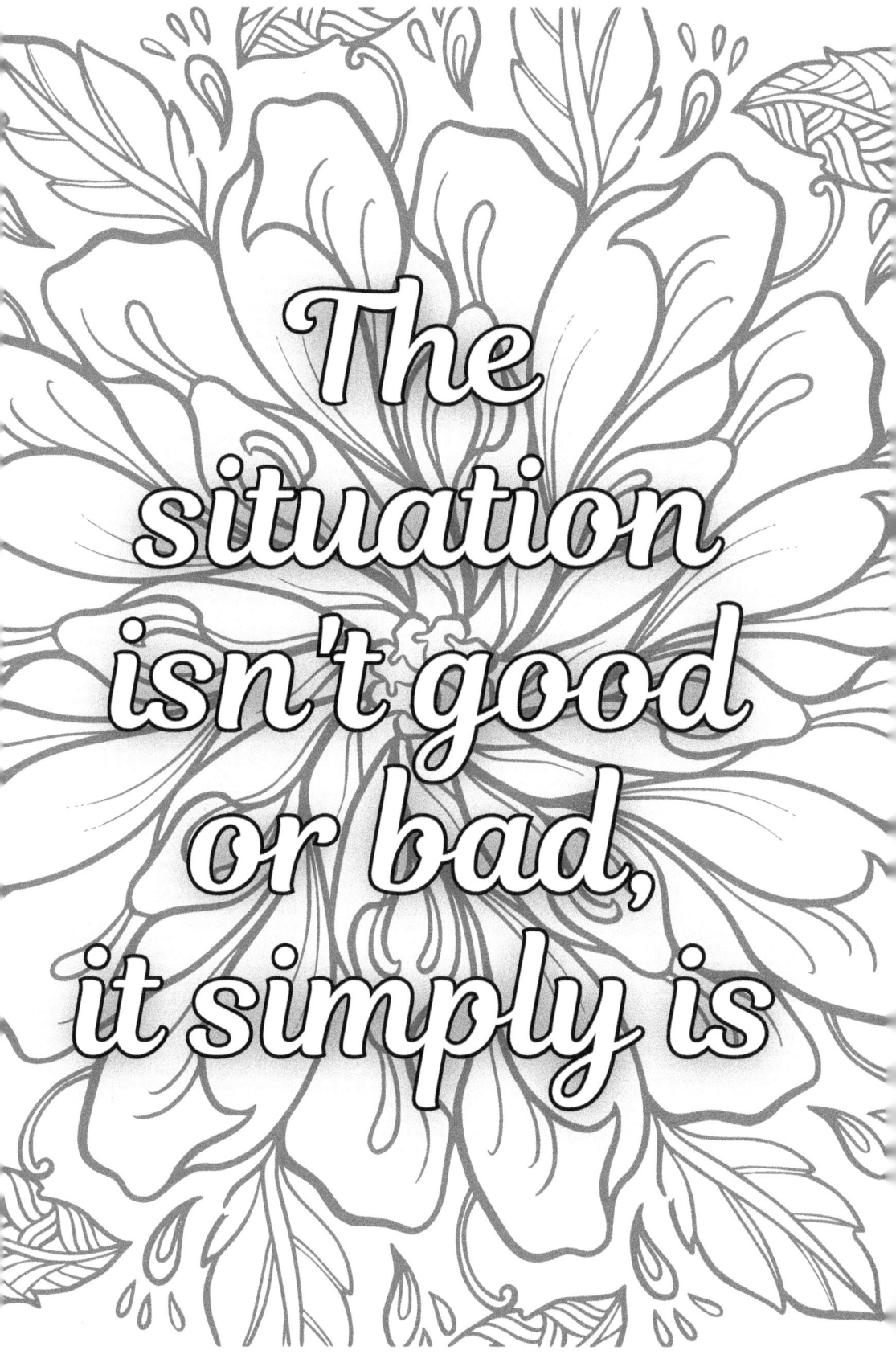

The
situation
isn't good
or bad,
it simply is

"As above, so below; as within, so without."

– Hermes Trismegistus

If I am mad at where I am, I need to stop making the same shitty choices and choose another path.

I am doing the best that I can, and that is enough

"We cannot change what
we are not aware of, and
once we are aware, we
cannot help but change."

- Sheryl Sandberg

I release all limiting
beliefs and negative
energy that hold me back
from my highest potential.

"I am a woman with thoughts and questions and shit to say.
I say if I'm beautiful.
I say if I'm strong.
You will not determine my story – I will."

– Amy Schumer

I am a badass who can handle anything that comes my way.

"When you realize how perfect everything is, you will tilt your head back and laugh at the sky."

– Buddha

I am guided by my intuition and trust that it will always lead me in the right direction.

"I am not a victim of my circumstances. I am a product of my decisions."

- Stephen Covey

I am stardust wrapped in a meat suit, housing a soul. I will get some fucking perspective.

"If you don't like the road you're walking, start paving another one."

– Dolly Parton

I create my own reality, however I want that magical shit to be.

"The best way to predict your future is to create it."

– Abraham Lincoln

I honour my ancestors and their wisdom, knowing that their guidance is always with me.

"I didn't get there by
wishing for it or hoping for
it, but by working for it."

– Estée Lauder

I am a co-creator with
the universe and
manifest my desires with
ease and grace.

"You yourself, as much as anybody in the entire universe, deserve your love and affection."

– Buddha

I connect with the energy of the earth and harness its power to manifest my goals.

"Believe you can and you're halfway there."

– Theodore Roosevelt

I embrace my flaws and quirks because they make me unique and fabulous.

"You are not a drop in the
ocean. You are the entire
ocean in a drop."

– Rumi

I am surrounded by magic
and miracles every day.

"Magic is believing in yourself, if you can do that, you can make anything happen."

- Johann Wolfgang von Goethe

I am grateful for all the magical experiences and opportunities that come my way, and I am excited for what's yet to come.

"The most beautiful thing we can experience is the mysterious. It is the source of all true art and science."

– Albert Einstein

I embrace my shadow self and integrate it with my light to create balance and wholeness.

"The power of imagination makes us infinite."

– John Muir

I can't clear muddy water by shaking the motherfucker, I have to be still.

"Every great dream begins with a dreamer.
Always remember, you have within you the strength, the patience, and the passion to reach for the stars to change the world."

- Harriet Tubman

I'm going to put my big girl pants on, I've got magical shit to do!

"The magic in new beginnings is truly the most powerful of them all."

– Josiyah Martin

I am unstoppable, and I will never let anyone or anything hold me back.

"If you have good thoughts they will shine out of your face like sunbeams and you will always look lovely."

– Roald Dahl

I will stop being so fucking hard on myself!

"The future belongs to those who believe in the beauty of their dreams."

– Eleanor Roosevelt

I embrace change and use it to grow and evolve into a better version of myself.

"The mind is everything.
What you think you
become."

– Buddha

I'm supernatural.
No one is a mere mortal.
I'm going to act like it!

Ready to go further on your spiritual journey?

There's always time and space to grow and expand.

Check out the members program portal below by scanning the QR code or jumping in at – members.newleafyourlife.com

MEMBERS PORTAL

www.ingramcontent.com/pod-product-compliance
Lightning Source LLC
Chambersburg PA
CBHW051513120626
46551CB00012B/904